Stand Up and Sing!

Pete Seeger, Folk Music, and the Path to Justice

To Julia Reich and James Reich,
who make the world a better place
—S. R.

For Plum
—A. G.

Stand Up and Sing!

Pete Seeger, Folk Music, and the Path to Justice

Susanna Reich • Illustrated by Adam Gustavson

Foreword by Peter Yarrow

BLOOMSBURY
NEW YORK LONDON OXFORD NEW DELHI SYDNEY

FOREWORD

For more than six decades, Pete Seeger has unquestionably been the inspiration and role model for folk singers such as Mary, Noel Paul, and me. It was he, more than anyone, who by example showed so many of us how to combine our music with our social/political consciousness and advocacies. Pete's great gift, even beyond his extraordinary singing and songwriting, was the fact that he fully lived the message of his music so that where his convictions went, there he stood: solidly, fearlessly, and unequivocally.

Early on, in the '50s, Pete refused to answer questions and "name names" before the House Un-American Activities Committee though he knew he would lose his livelihood, be blacklisted, and be sentenced to jail (all of which occurred). He was, in a word, the embodiment of courage in the face of great evil. Yet, astonishingly, his love of humankind and his creative and personal light continued to grow brighter and brighter through the years.

Mary Travers used to call our trio "Seeger's Raiders" and, following Pete's example, we put our hearts and personal selves where our convictions lay, as did so many of our other contemporaries in the context of the civil rights movement, the Anti–Vietnam War Movement, and many grassroots struggles thereafter.

As the years pass, whenever you hear a folk singer singing her or his songs at a march or demonstration, whenever you hear a song that in plainspoken words tells the story of the hopes, the trials, or the aspirations of ordinary human beings, you'll be listening, in part, to Pete as his spirit travels beyond his time on earth. In these times, there is so much that divides us, so much greed, narcissism, and other terrible threats to the dream of creating a caring, just, and peaceful society—and to the survival of our planet. What Pete taught us is how to keep on keepin' on, how to keep on singing, how to not become cynical, and how to turn challenge and adversity into greater determination and love for one another. That was Pete.

Peter Yarrow

Pete Seeger plucks and strums the banjo. His warm, high voice floats over the crowd. Heads begin to bob and toes to tap. Suddenly Pete stops.

"Now, even if you never heard this song before, you can sing it with me," he says.

He calls out the words. Gradually, quiet folks find their courage, and the chorus of voices grows. Soon nearly everyone has joined in, and Pete's voice is ringing out in harmony. His fast-picking fingers fly over the strings as his boots bang out the rhythm.

"Everybody, sing it!" he cries.

When the music ends, people leap to their feet, clapping, whooping, and whistling.

Pete Seeger was born in 1919, with music in his bones. As a toddler he'd toot, shake, and bang on the instruments Mother left all over the apartment, his little knees jiggling and his hips a-wiggling.

As time went on, Pete's parents disagreed about a lot of things. When they separated, he was at boarding school in Connecticut. There he felt shy—except when playing songs with silly words and clever rhymes on his ukulele.

Summers, he lived with his brothers and father in his grandparents' barn.

"Every meal we sang our hearts out," said Pete's brother John.

Pete drew, played in the woods, and built model boats and airplanes. He read about Native Americans and loved the idea that in some tribes, everything was shared.

"I decided that was the way to live: no rich, no poor. If there was food, everyone ate; if there was no food, everyone went hungry."

Maybe he'd live in the forest for the rest of his life!

In high school Pete started a shoeshine business and a newspaper. He was angry when the school wouldn't let him print an article about a pet snake loose in the dorm. They said the story would make the school look bad. Pete thought the truth was important.

One thing that always rang true for Pete was music. He had so much fun fooling around on a teacher's banjo that he begged his mother to let him get his own.

I would like to buy a big banjo, he wrote.

Did you receive my package, the sweater, and underwear? she replied.

Yes, yes, yes, wrote Pete. *Please, Mother, can I have that banjo?*

When she agreed, Pete bought a used four-string banjo with savings from his allowance.

Back home in New York City, Father and his new wife, Ruth, had trouble paying their bills. In 1929 the stock market had crashed and the Great Depression had begun. Millions lost their jobs and their homes. Families went hungry. To Pete, it didn't seem fair that some folks were rich and some had nothing.

Father took Pete to poor neighborhoods to see the suffering caused by hard times. Together they marched in parades for working people and went to parties where folk singers shared protest songs. At one concert, the performers and the audience sang together about workers' rights—thousands of voices united by a common purpose, demanding equality, justice, and respect. Pete was so impressed, he went back to school and wrote a paper about it.

The near-empty cupboards at home made a deep impression too.

FREE
SOUP, COFFEE, AND DOUGHNUTS FOR THE UNEMPLOYED

Before he started college, Pete and his family drove to a music and dance festival in Asheville, North Carolina. Traveling through the mountains, Pete saw barefoot children dressed in rags, peeking from the doorways of tumbledown shacks, and felt like he was "visiting a foreign country." But when he heard the rippling rhythms of the five-string banjo, it was like coming home. He couldn't wait to get his hands on one!

Soon Pete learned to fingerpick a banjo. Listening to records over and over, he tried to imitate what he heard—rhythm, melody, chords, and words.

"And I, born in New York City, started learning songs of Kentucky miners, Wisconsin lumberjacks, and Texas farmers," he said.

At college Pete couldn't stop talking about workers' strikes and unions, the civil war in Spain, and the Nazis in Germany. He talked so much that he didn't do his homework. He lost his scholarship and had to drop out of school.

Jobs were hard to find. One day Pete played his banjo on the street and earned seventy-five cents—enough in those days to buy eight loaves of bread! Eventually he went to work for family friend Alan Lomax, who collected and recorded folk songs for the Library of Congress.

Music echoed through the Seeger home day and night. Spirituals, work songs, dance tunes, game songs, lullabies, love songs, ballads, field hollers, blues, and chain-gang chants—Pete fell in love with them all. When he wasn't helping Alan organize songs, he was practicing the banjo.

"He played all night, and he played all day, and after a while you wanted to ship him off somewhere," said Alan's sister Bess.

Through Alan, Pete met Woody Guthrie, who'd just written "This Land Is Your Land." "I learned so many different things from Woody that I can hardly count them," Pete said.

In a few hours Woody could write a song about the day's news or spin a tale about the countryside he was traveling through. Pete was thrilled when Woody let him "tag along" on a trip to Texas, playing at union meetings along the way.

In Oklahoma City the crowd included oil workers and their wives and children—as well as some men lined up in the back of the room, fixing for a fight. Fearing violence, the organizer called on Pete and Woody to play. Soon the families were singing, and the men in the back slunk off.

That night Pete saw that music could fill a room with peace and harmony—even if he still couldn't figure out how to sing and play banjo at the same time!

Living again in New York City, Pete practiced and practiced.

"He would get up in the morning, and before he'd eat or anything, he'd reach for the banjo and begin to play, sitting on his bed in his underwear," said a roommate.

Pete and some friends formed a group, the Almanac Singers. Word got around that they could really get an audience fired up, and within six months they'd performed for twenty thousand people at Madison Square Garden. Before long they were singing for autoworkers in Detroit and longshoremen in San Francisco, inspiring union members to believe that someday jobs would be safer and workers better paid.

On tour the Almanacs slept on people's couches or in cheap hotels, including one with "enormous cockroaches in every room." The following winter in New York City, they couldn't afford to heat their apartment. Pete didn't mind the cold. It felt good to be making a difference in the world.

When Toshi-Aline Ohta began helping the Almanacs alphabetize their song files, Pete paid attention—to Toshi, not the files. She was smart, creative, and "peppery."

The Second World War had started, and Pete was drafted. He married Toshi and was shipped out to the South Pacific. Far from home under the swaying palm trees, the wounded soldiers could sing with Pete and forget their injuries for a little while.

After the war, Pete threw himself into the "singing union movement." Music, he thought, helped folks feel strong and connected as they fought for fair pay and better working conditions. He and Toshi started a family and in 1949 bought land in Beacon, New York. High on a hill overlooking the Hudson River, they started to build a log cabin. Then a scary thing happened.

Pete, Woody, and the African American singer Paul Robeson were appearing at an outdoor concert near Peekskill, New York. Busloads of police arrived, expecting trouble. Some folks were angry that whites and blacks were performing on the same stage. They said it was un-American to believe in workers' rights and racial equality.

The concert went off without a hitch, but as Pete and his family were leaving, a rock smashed through their car window. On the road ahead, men were throwing stones at every car. The police refused to help. All of the Seegers' car windows were shattered.

Later Pete found two rocks inside the car and cemented them into his fireplace. They'd always remind him how important it was to stand up for his beliefs—and to never stop singing.

That winter Pete and his new singing group, the Weavers, began performing at a New York City club. Audiences greeted songs like "If I Had a Hammer" with wild applause. By summertime the Weavers' recording of "Goodnight, Irene" was a number-one hit.

Despite the group's success, Pete was unhappy. He wanted to sing for—and with—average working folks. Instead he was staying in fancy hotels and performing in glittering clubs. He missed his family and his log cabin in the woods.

The Weavers had bigger problems. Powerful people in the government said their songs about the rights of workers and African Americans were unpatriotic.

Soon clubs stopped inviting the group to perform, and stores refused to sell their records. The Weavers had been *blacklisted*. Unable to make a living, the group took a break. Hard times lay ahead.

In 1955 Pete was called into court by some congressmen who didn't think he was a loyal American. Pete refused to answer their questions in the way they wanted. The threat of prison would hang over his head for the next seven years.

Meanwhile the civil rights movement was picking up steam. On a trip to Tennessee in 1957, Pete introduced Dr. Martin Luther King Jr. to the song "We Shall Overcome."

"That song really sticks with you, doesn't it?" Dr. King said.

"We Shall Overcome" spread throughout the country. In churches and community halls, at civil rights gatherings and protest marches, people stood arm in arm, their voices forming a bond of hope and determination.

During these years Pete could barely make a living. Still, he loved to perform, especially for children—he'd moo like a cow and honk like a goose, and the kids would giggle in delight. Pete felt like Johnny Appleseed, spreading folk music seeds song by song and child by child.

Eventually the seeds Pete planted began to sprout. Young folk singers popped up from coast to coast, and some of his songs became hits. Together he and Toshi answered bushel baskets full of fan mail. Pete let off steam by chopping wood and sailing the Hudson River.

Best of all, in 1962 his legal problems were settled. He was still blacklisted—concerts might be canceled at the last minute, and no commercial television show would have him on. But Pete thought he'd never do anything in music more important than teaching young Americans the folk tradition.

He didn't realize there was still important work to come.

In 1965 Dr. King invited Pete and Toshi to join him in Alabama. African Americans were being denied the right to vote, and blacks and whites were marching together in peaceful protest. Risking their lives in the dangerous struggle for civil rights, the marchers sometimes felt afraid. Singing kept them strong.

By day, as the crowd walked the highway from Selma to Montgomery, "song after song" rose into the air. At night people huddled around flickering campfires, singing to keep up their courage. As voices swelled in the darkness, Pete slipped from one campfire to another, jotting down the words of songs so he'd always remember them.

Within a few months of the march, President Lyndon Johnson signed a new law that helped guarantee all Americans the right to vote. No longer would the country tolerate hatred and injustice, he said.

"And," he added, "we *shall* overcome."

Pete and Dr. King dreamed of peace, but in the 1960s the United States was at war in faraway Vietnam. Many Americans wondered if the president was leading the country in the wrong direction.

When hundreds of thousands of teenage boys were drafted into the army, protests rocked the college campuses where Pete performed. He wrote a song, "Waist Deep in the Big Muddy," in which an army captain leads soldiers across a river. The water gets deeper and deeper, but the captain won't stop, and eventually he drowns. People who heard the song understood that Pete was criticizing President Johnson for taking the nation deeper into war.

In 1967 Pete was invited to appear on national television for the first time in seventeen years. After taping the show, Pete was furious when he saw it on TV. They had cut out "Big Muddy"!

"What they did was wrong," he told a newspaper reporter.

Luckily, a few months later he was invited back on TV, and this time seven million people saw him perform "Big Muddy." Still the Vietnam War ground on. It would be seven more years before the last American soldier came home.

Pete was angry and discouraged, especially after Dr. King was shot and killed in 1968. He began to wonder if singing really did have the power to change the world. How could he lead people in song if he didn't have hope for the future?

If you despair, what happens to the many, many people like myself who look to you constantly for hope? wrote a fan.

Little did he know he'd find the answer right in his own backyard.

Sailing on the Hudson near his home during the 1960s, Pete often saw garbage in the water. People were treating the river like a dump! With Toshi and some friends he hatched a plan to build a sloop—an old-fashioned boat with a mast more than one hundred feet tall—that would sail the river and inspire people to clean it up.

At a shipyard in Maine, Pete and other volunteers hauled iron and lumber, rope and canvas, nails and paint and tar. Slowly, the boat took shape.

On a hot June day in 1969, *Clearwater* set sail for New York City. There the mayor stood on deck while television newsmen thrust microphones at Pete. Then the boat that Pete called "a symphony of curves" headed up the Hudson. It's been her home ever since.

A clean river, a peaceful planet, a living wage—as Pete got older, he continued to sing, to protest, and to inspire people to speak out for their beliefs. When President Barack Obama took office in 2009, Pete led four hundred thousand people in singing "This Land Is Your Land" at the Lincoln Memorial in Washington, DC. The civil rights movement had come a long way, but Pete knew the struggle for equality would go on.

Pete passed away in 2014, but his work isn't done. For in times of war, the world needs peace. In times of hatred, the world needs love. In times of injustice, the world needs truth. And wherever people gather in the name of freedom, they find strength and courage in song.

Today on the Hudson River, when *Clearwater*'s sails fill with wind and singing rises from her deck, she tells a story about standing tall, binding people together in friendship, and lifting them up with the power of music. If you listen closely, you just might hear the voice of Pete Seeger.

"When one person taps out a beat . . . [or] three people discover a harmony . . . or a crowd joins in on a chorus as though to raise the ceiling a few feet higher, then they also know there is hope for the world."

AUTHOR'S NOTE

My work on this book began with a sense of personal connection. Like Pete, I grew up in a family with a tradition of political activism. Each of us had a parent who was a musicologist by profession. We shared a love for the Hudson Valley, where I've lived most of my life, and I heard him perform many times, most memorably at one of the first Clearwater festivals. It was 1969, the year the sloop was launched, and by the end of the day I was so charged with energy that I walked the five miles home.

Of course, lives are shaped not just by personal history but by political, economic, and social forces. Both Pete and I came of age in times of turmoil. As a child he found solace and guidance in Ernest Thompson Seton's books on nature and Native Americans, and as a teenager his political consciousness was awakened by the Great Depression, the union movement, and the rise of fascism in Europe. My childhood, in turn, was defined by the tumultuous 1960s, with its civil rights struggle, political assassinations, war in Vietnam, environmental and youth movements, and the folk music revival that owed so much to Pete.

Pete inherited musical traditions from Bascom Lamar Lunsford, Samantha Bumgarner, Woody Guthrie, Lead Belly, and many others. His ancestors included Revolutionary War patriots and nineteenth-century abolitionists, and his father and stepmother had a profound influence on his thinking about music, culture, and politics. As I researched this book, I came to understand why Pete saw himself as a link in a chain. It's a chain in which music and social responsibility are intertwined, one that began long before he was born and will continue now that he's gone. This book is meant to be a link in that chain.

"A folk song in a book is like a picture of a bird in midflight," Pete once wrote. "The bird was moving before the picture was taken, and continued flying afterwards." So, too, the subject of a biography. In compressing Pete's story into a picture book, there was much I had to leave out. I hope what remains is a colorful, accurate, and inspiring portrait of an extraordinary man.

QUOTES

"Now, even if you never heard," and "Everybody, sing it!": Pete Seeger, in live performance, *Pete Seeger: The Power of Song*.

"Every meal": John Seeger, interviewed in *Pete Seeger: The Power of Song*.

"I decided": *Pete Seeger: In His Own Words*, 314.

"I would like to buy": letter from Pete Seeger to Constance Seeger, Fall 1932, *Pete Seeger: In His Own Words*, 8.

"Did you receive" and "Yes, yes, yes": correspondence between Constance and Pete Seeger, quoted in Dunaway, 42.

"visiting a foreign country": Pete Seeger, quoted in Tick, 239.

"And I, born in New York City": *Pete Seeger: In His Own Words*, 12.

"He played all night": Bess Lomax Hawes, quoted in Dunaway, 65.

"I learned so many different things": *Pete Seeger: In His Own Words*, 52.

"tag along": Pete Seeger, interviewed in *Pete Seeger: The Power of Song*.

"He would get up": Millard Lampell, quoted in Dunaway, 89.

"enormous cockroaches": letter from Pete Seeger to Millard Lampell, October 1, 1987, *Pete Seeger: In His Own Words*, 20.

"peppery": *Where Have All the Flowers Gone*, 45.

"singing union movement": *Pete Seeger: In His Own Words*, xvii.

"That song really sticks with you": Pete Seeger, interviewed in *Pete Seeger: The Power of Song*.

"song after song": *Pete Seeger: In His Own Words*, 121.

"And we *shall* overcome": President Lyndon Baines Johnson, in speech to Congress introducing bill that became Voting Rights Act of 1965.

"What they did": Pete Seeger, quoted in Gent, George. "Seeger Accuses CBS Over Song," *New York Times*, September 13, 1967, 95.

"If you despair": fan letter to Pete Seeger, quoted in Dunaway, 334.

"a symphony of curves": *Pete Seeger: In His Own Words*, 153.

"When one person": Pete Seeger, interviewed in *Pete Seeger: The Power of Song*.

"A folk song in a book": *Pete Seeger: In His Own Words*, 68.

SELECTED SOURCES

Books

Dunaway, David King. *How Can I Keep from Singing?: The Ballad of Pete Seeger*. New York: Villard, 2008.

Pescatello, Ann M. *Charles Seeger: A Life in American Music*. Pittsburgh: University of Pittsburgh Press, 1992.

Seeger, Pete. *Pete Seeger: In His Own Words*. Boulder: Paradigm Publishers, 2012.

Seeger, Pete. *Where Have All the Flowers Gone: A Singalong Memoir*. Bethlehem, PA: A Sing Out Publication, 1993.

Tick, Judith. *Ruth Crawford Seeger: A Composer's Search for American Music*. New York: Oxford University Press, 1997.

Wilkinson, Alec. *The Protest Singer: An Intimate Portrait of Pete Seeger*. New York: Alfred A. Knopf, 2009.

Films

The Pete and Toshi Seeger Film Collection. American Folklife Center, Library of Congress.

Pete Seeger: Live in Australia 1963. Acorn Media/Reelin' in the Years Productions, 2009.

Pete Seeger: The Power of Song. The Weinstein Company Home Entertainment, 2008.

'Til the River Runs Clear. PBS Home Video, 2007.

The Weavers: Wasn't That a Time! New York: MGM/UA Home Video, 1981.

Radio and TV Interviews

"Pete Seeger." *The Colbert Report*, Comedy Central, August 6, 2012.

"Pete Seeger Recalls the 1949 Peekskill Riot Where He and Paul Robeson Were Attacked." democracynow.org, February 4, 2004.

"Pete Seeger Remembers His Late Wife, Toshi, Sings Civil Rights Anthem 'We Shall Overcome.'" democracynow.org, August 9, 2013.

"Seeger in His Own Words." *The Brian Lehrer Show*, WNYC, July 18, 2012.

"We Shall Overcome: An Hour with Legendary Folk Singer & Activist Pete Seeger." democracynow.org, February 4, 2004.

Recordings

In a career spanning seven decades, Pete recorded dozens of albums. Here are some songs to look for:

"Turn! Turn! Turn!"

"If I Had a Hammer"

"Where Have All the Flowers Gone?"

"We Shall Overcome"

"Wimoweh"

"Little Boxes"

"Waist Deep in the Big Muddy"

"Guantanamera"

"Bring 'Em Home"

"Goodnight, Irene"

Websites

www.clearwater.org

www.rememberingpeteseeger.org

Pete Seeger, 1955

Pete Seeger, 2009

First published in the United States of America in March 2017 by Bloomsbury Children's Books
www.bloomsbury.com

Bloomsbury is a registered trademark of Bloomsbury Publishing Plc

For information about permission to reproduce selections from this book, write to
Permissions, Bloomsbury Children's Books, 1385 Broadway, New York, New York 10018
Bloomsbury books may be purchased for business or promotional use. For information on bulk purchases
please contact Macmillan Corporate and Premium Sales Department at specialmarkets@macmillan.com

Library of Congress Cataloging-in-Publication Data
Names: Reich, Susanna. | Gustavson, Adam.
Title: Stand up and sing! : Pete Seeger, folk music, and the path to justice / by Susanna Reich ; illustrated by Adam Gustavson.
Description: New York : Bloomsbury, 2017.
Identifiers: LCCN 2016022360 (print)
ISBN 978-0-8027-3812-7 (hardcover)
Subjects: LCSH: Seeger, Pete, 1919–2014—Juvenile literature. | Folk singers—United States—Biography—Juvenile literature.
Classification: LCC ML3930.S42 R45 2017 (print) | DDC 782.42162/130092 [B]—dc23
LC record available at https://lccn.loc.gov/2016022360

Artwork created using gouache, watercolor, colored pencil, and/or oil paint on paper, with little bits of Adobe Photoshop
Typeset in Adobe Caslon Pro • Book design by Colleen Andrews
Printed in China by Leo Paper Products, Heshan, Guangdong
2 4 6 8 10 9 7 5 3 1

All papers used by Bloomsbury Publishing, Inc., are natural, recyclable products made from wood grown in well-managed forests.
The manufacturing processes conform to the environmental regulations of the country of origin.